# What is a biography?

A biography is the true story of a real person's life. Most biographies are about famous people. Some are about ordinary people. They can be about someone who lived long ago, or they can be about someone who is still alive today.

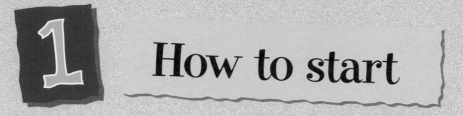

# How to start

Choose a person you like and admire to write about. You will have to start by finding out all about them, and it's much more fun finding things out about someone you're really interested in.

# How to Write a Biography

*written by* Jenny Alexander
*illustrated by* Jeff Anderson

Vincent van Gogh

June Stevens

DAVID BECKHAM

# Contents

David Beckham

Vincent van Gogh

Auntie June

# ② Finding the facts

A biography is non-fiction, so it must only contain facts. Here are some of the facts you will need to find out:

- when the person was born

- what interesting things he or she has done

- if your person is not still alive, when he or she died.

OF BIRTH

ELIZ. 2 CH. 20

...TIFICATE

...ame and Surname _June Anne Stevens_

...ex _Female_

Date of Birth _2 May 1951_

Place of Birth { Registration District _Chigwell_  CHIGWELL

Sub-district

I, _PBSwanson_ Registrar of Births and Deaths in the for the sub-district of _Chigwell_ CHIGWELL do hereby Registration District of _CHIGWELL_ certify that the above particulars have been compiled from an entry in a register in my custody.

Date _30.5.1951_    _PBSwanson_ Registrar of Births and Deaths.

CAUTION:— Any person who (1) falsifies any of the particulars on this certificate, or (2) uses a falsified certificate as true, knowing it to be false, is liable to prosecution.

# BECKHAM!
## Ace striker makes it another winner for Manchester United

If the person you are writing about is famous, you will probably get most of your facts from books. Look in your school library. If there aren't any books about the person you have chosen there, look in the library in your town or village. Ask the librarian to help you.

Look on the Internet. See if the person you are writing about has a website, or belongs to an organisation that has a website. For example, there might be something about a famous footballer in the club's web pages.

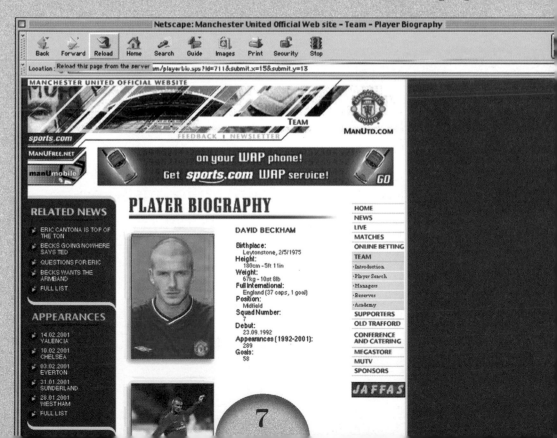

Look up the person you have chosen on a reference CD-ROM or in an encyclopedia. Look for articles in newspapers and magazines. Some famous people, like footballers and pop stars, are often in the papers.

Dear Sam

Thank you
I would like

I wish you
and hope

If the person is alive, write a letter to him or her. Explain that you are writing a biography. Choose one or two questions to ask. If you ask, some famous people will send photos.

If you are writing about someone you know, like your auntie, talk to her about her life. Ask her whether she has got any photos you could borrow or photocopy.

Auntie June, age 12

This is me getting my Collector's badge at Brownies. That's how it all started really.

Can I borrow it for my biography?

Talk to other people who know your person too. They may also have some old photos you could use.

Your Auntie June only thought of opening this café because she had so many pictures of the Queen. She didn't have enough room to display them all in her house. This place was just an old shed when she bought it.

Have you got a photo of it?

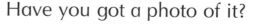

11

# Finding the pictures

Here are some of the ways you can get pictures for your biography.

(1) Ask the person for a photo.

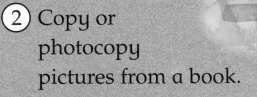

(2) Copy or photocopy pictures from a book.

(3) Print pictures from websites or reference CDs.

(4) Cut out pictures from newspapers or magazines.

(5) Look in shops for cards and postcards. For example, if your person is an artist, there may be postcards of his or her work. If your person comes from your town, you could get a postcard of where he or she was born.

# 4 Choosing what to put in

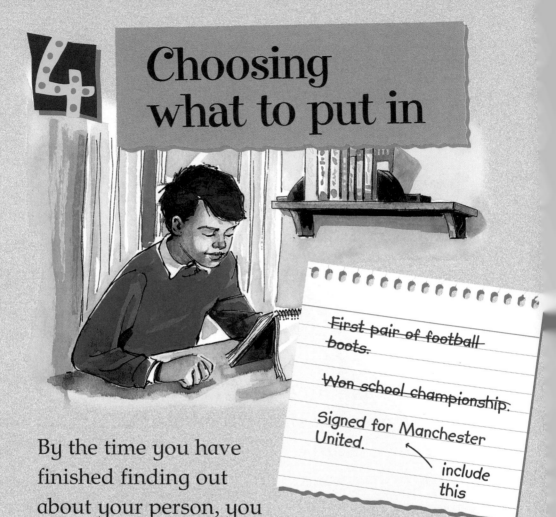

First pair of football boots.

Won school championship.

Signed for Manchester United. ← include this

By the time you have finished finding out about your person, you will know lots of things about him or her. If you put everything you know in your biography, it will probably be too long. It might also be boring to read. So just choose the things that seem most important and interesting.

You may have too many pictures, too.
First, decide which one is best for your cover.
It should be a picture of the person you are
writing about. Then choose one or two more
pictures taken, if possible, at different stages
of his or her life.

this one
on
cover

Choose one or two pictures of places. For example, you could have a picture of where your person was born, or of the countryside he or she loved. If you are writing about an artist, try to include a few examples of his or her work.

This is my favourite van Gogh painting.

# 5 | Writing it

First, make a list of important dates. Start with the year your person was born. Put in some of the the important things that happened. Finish with the year the person died, or if the person is still alive, the present day.

### Auntie June's Biography

| | |
|---|---|
| 1951 | Auntie June born |
| 1954 | nearly died of measles |
| 1966 | left school |
| 1968 | started working in Dutton's bakers |
| 1972 | married Uncle Harold |
| 1991 | opened 'Tea with the Queen' teashop |
| Today | still serving the best cup of tea in Ashton! |

Put in important things that were happening in the world, too.

## Auntie June's Biography

| | |
|---|---|
| 1951 | Auntie June born |
| 1952 | Queen Elizabeth II crowned |
| 1954 | nearly died of measles |
| 1966 | left school |
| 1966 | Royal visit to Ashton |
| 1968 | started working in Dutton's bakers |
| 1972 | married Uncle Harold |
| 1977 | Queen Elizabeth's Silver Jubilee |
| 1991 | opened 'Tea with the Queen' teashop |
| Today | still serving the best cup of tea in Ashton! |

# David Beckham

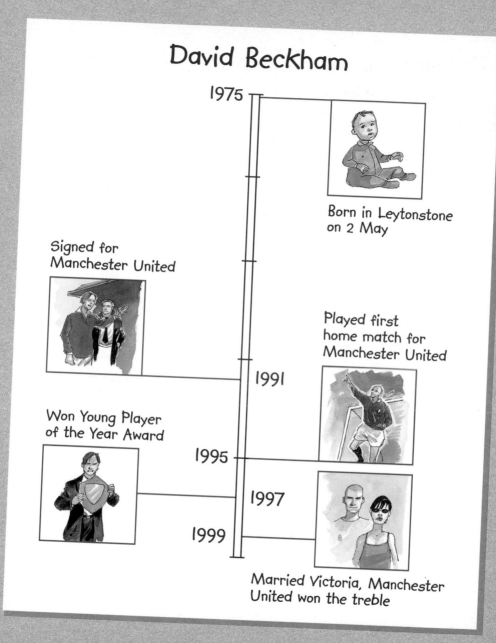

1975 — Born in Leytonstone on 2 May

Signed for Manchester United

1991 — Played first home match for Manchester United

Won Young Player of the Year Award

1995

1997

1999 — Married Victoria, Manchester United won the treble

If you prefer, make a timeline instead of a list.

Once you have made a timeline or a list of dates, writing a biography is easy. The timeline or list of dates is like a writing plan. All you have to do now is to describe what happened in the order it happened.

Auntie June's childhood

Auntie June was born in 1951. When she was three she nearly died of

van Gogh painted lots of pictures of sunflowers.

Remember to write a line under each picture to say what it is.

# 6 Finishing off

Vincent van Gogh

1853, born in the Netherlands

1890, died in France

When you have written all about your person's life, produce a map to show where the person was born. If the person is dead, mark where he or she died. Or, if the person is still alive, mark where they live now.

Finally, put in a list of the books you have used, and the people who have helped you. This shows your work is based on facts. It may also help readers who have enjoyed your biography, because it tells them where they can find out more.

DAVID BECKHAM

June Stevens

Vincent van Gogh

# Writing a biography is fun because ...

- you find out all about someone you are interested in

- you don't have to make anything up, so it's easy to write

- it includes interesting things like timelines and maps

- other people will enjoy reading it.

**Why not give it a try?**

# Index